NOMINATED FOR:

THE 2009 SUSAN SMITH BLACKBURN PRIZE
THE 2009 GOVERNOR GENERAL'S LITERARY AWARD FOR DRAMA
THE 2009 CANADIAN AUTHOR'S ASSOCIATION CAROL BOLT AWARD
THE 2008 DORA MAVOR MOORE AWARD FOR BEST NEW PLAY,
GENERAL CATEGORY

"Hannah Moscovitch [is] a young and quite irritatingly talented writer…" —Paul Isaacs, *Eye Weekly*

"…an emotional and intellectual focus that seamlessly travels across continents and about 40 years of history."
—Kamal Al-Solaylee, *Globe and Mail*

"…a Holocaust play with a difference."
—Jon Kaplan, *NOW Magazine*

"…those looking for real theatre, the kind that stretches your heart and your brain, will be well-rewarded."
—Richard Ouzounian, *Toronto Star*

"[Moscovitch is] not afraid to plunge right through areas that others might consider poor taste in order to come out the other side in search of a deeper truth." —*Variety*

"… important and brave work… a must-see show, by any definition." —*Fresh Daily Theatre Review*

EAST OF BERLIN

EAST **OF BERLIN**
HANNAH MOSCOVITCH

PLAYWRIGHTS CANADA PRESS
TORONTO

Playwrights Canada Press
202-269 Richmond St. W.
Toronto, ON M5V 1X1
416.703.0013 · info@playwrightscanada.com · www.playwrightscanada.com

We acknowledge the financial support of the Canada Council for the Arts, the Ontario Arts Council, the Ontario Media Development Corporation, and the Government of Canada through the Canada Book Fund for our publishing activities.

 Canada Council for the Arts · Conseil des Arts du Canada  ONTARIO ARTS COUNCIL CONSEIL DES ARTS DE L'ONTARIO

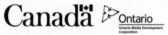 Canada · Ontario Ontario Media Development Corporation

Cover design by Monnet Design
Typesetting by Blake Sproule

LIBRARY AND ARCHIVES CANADA CATALOGUING IN PUBLICATION
Moscovitch, Hannah
East of Berlin / Hannah Moscovitch.

A play.
ISBN 978-0-88754-849-9

I. Title.

PS8626.O837E28 2009   C812'.6   C2009-901460-2

First edition: May 2009
Third printing: November 2012
Printed and bound in Canada by Imprimerie Gauvin, Gatineau

To my father, Allan Moscovitch

Playwright's Notes

A note on the title: the word "East" was used by the Nazis to refer to the genocide of the Jews. The official party line was that Jewish communities were being "resettled in the East." This euphemism entered into the language of Berlin Jews during the war. The word "East" was used to refer to the death camps, and "to go East" of the city signified "going to your death."

A note for future productions: when I wrote the script, I sought to create the possibility for a tense relationship between Rudi and the audience. I envisioned this relationship as the most important of the play.

CHARACTERS

Sarah (speaks with a slight New York accent)
Hermann
Rudi

East of Berlin was first produced by Tarragon Theatre, October 16 to November 24, 2007, with the following company:

SARAH Diana Donnelly
HERMANN Paul Dunn
RUDI Brendan Gall

Directed by Alisa Palmer
Set and Costume Design by Camilla Koo
Lighting Design by Michael Walton
Music and Sound Design by John Gzowski
Stage Managed by Leigh McClymont
Fight Direction by James Binkley
Script Coordinated by Maureen Gualtieri

Do not hold against us the sins of the fathers; may your mercy come quickly to meet us, for we are in desperate need.

—Psalm 79: 7–9

It's 1970. RUDI is in the front hallway outside his father's study, in his family home in Asunción, Paraguay. He is trying to light a cigarette. It's difficult because his hands are shaking. RUDI stops trying to light the cigarette for a moment and controls himself. Then he lights his cigarette. He takes a drag. He speaks to the audience.

RUDI   I used to smoke, in Paraguay. It's a disgusting habit, I know. I'm returning to old habits here.

Beat.

I grew up here, in Paraguay. Fucking Paraguay.

Beat.

At the airport, the customs official had Band-Aids on his hands that were crusted over with dirt and pus. I kept looking at them as he went through my suitcase. Also, he was smoking and the ash kept falling onto my clothes.

Beat.

I've been away too long; I've been in Germany too long, if these things disgust me.

Beat.

(*referring to the cigarette*) Thank God for... I bought these at the airport and I just fucking love them.

Beat.

When I lived here, in Paraguay, I smoked packs and packs of cigarettes. They—I don't know—helped me, somehow. Now I only smoke to mark significant events in my life.

Beat.

Births.

Beat.

Deaths.

Beat.

Paradigm shifts.

Beat.

When I get laid, I smoke.

Beat.

Prodigal returns. To countries of origin. Paraguay. Although, I wasn't actually born here. I'm not Latin American; well, look at me.

Beat.

No. I was born in a little hospital, in Berlin. In 1945. *Right* as my father was losing the war.

RUDI takes a drag of his cigarette. He regards the audience.

That's right. My father lost the war, so he must... be... a...

Beat.

Cigarette?

Beat.

I can give you a moment to take that in. I've spent my whole life trying to take it in, so, please.

RUDI turns away, smokes.

(singing) "Deutschland, Deutschland, über alles, Über alles in der Welt." *(turning back to the audience)* Do you want to meet him? He's... here, he's in here, in his study, if you'd like to meet him? I'm going to go in there, in a minute, and... say hello, let him know I'm here, in Paraguay, in his house, let him know I've come home. Right after I... smoke this cigarette.

Beat.

He's been here since the late forties. I mean, not in his study, in South America.

Beat.

I still don't know who provided us with the emigration papers. I think there was an invitation from the government of Argentina. I was ten months old at the time. I have my German passport, a picture of me as a baby and the name "Otto Henrick" printed on it. Who the fuck is Otto Henrick, I'd really like to know. Well, or, maybe I wouldn't.

Beat.

There was a very pretty little apartment in Argentina. I liked my nanny there, her tits were huge, and she was always vacuuming, I found the sound soothing.

Beat.

At one point a house by the sea, a beach; Chile, I think. There were these girls in these—I think they were meant to be attractive, or, at least, suggestive—grass skirts. When they would come by the beach my mother would put her hand over my eyes.

Beat.

In Colombia, ah, now this you'll like, my father's military jacket. When we arrived in Colombia, the house was flooded, a burst pipe, I think. We left all of our packages and suitcases in the front hallway. My father's military jacket was lying out, so I tried it on. My father caught me at it. I thought he was going to be angry with me, but he wasn't. He kept saying, "So you like my jacket!"

Beat.

And on and on like that. A series of Latin American countries, a series of Latin American sympathizers. All financed by ODESSA. Not familiar with it? That's the organization that helped people like my father disappear.

Beat.

At some point we settled down, we stayed here. In Paraguay. But, don't imagine we tried to fit in. Oh no. In the middle of this colossal South American sewer, a small, shining German oasis. A whole expatriate community here, Third Reich refugees, Germans, Austrians, there was even a newspaper, *Die Morgenpost*. We had our own school, and our own beer hall, and most of the time we pretended that Hitler didn't lose.

Beat.

I barely spoke Spanish. Well, no, I spoke Spanish. I did speak Spanish. I tend to exaggerate. It's another habit. I get the exaggeration and the smoking from my mother. Our house, there was always smoke drifting out of the ashtrays, and my mother would be going on and on about how the neighbours were going to hand us over to the Russians. Or, after Eichmann, to the Israelis.

Beat.

What I get from my father? Well.

Beat.

It strikes me as stupid, even now, that I didn't realize, that I didn't put it together. That I spent so many years leading an ordinary life here. On the other hand, life seemed so ordinary. My father had his business, we were well off, big house, cars, servants. Nothing ever struck me as...

Beat.

Children. They have such a remarkable capacity for either accepting their circumstances, or dying. Who said that? I hope it wasn't Hitler, sometimes I quote him accidentally.

Beat.

I knew there was something, some part of the war that wasn't spoken about. If I asked too many questions about the war, my father shook his head at me. But then, if I asked too many questions about Latin girls, I got the same response.

Beat.

And my father, himself, was so very...

Beat.

He had a set of stock phrases he liked to repeat, such as, "You know we eat dinner at seven." "You know we don't walk on the lawn." He wore the same black suits. He had an incredibly methodical way of cleaning his nails.

Beat.

My parents' bed was up against my wall, and I would hear it creaking. It creaked sixteen times at exactly nine o'clock at night, my whole childhood, that's how boring he was, sixteen thrusts once a week, and that was it. That was my father.

Beat.

If you met him, you'd think, there's one of those bureaucrat types whose whole lives can be summed up in a few sentences.

Beat.

The point is, it wasn't until my late teens, seventeen, that a schoolmate let something slip. His name was Hermann, this schoolmate. Hermann was a bit of a... well. He was... well. Hermann was an aesthete, an intellectual. He was very good at school, he was always bored in class and rolling his eyes. He read Rilke and the beat poets and chain-smoked cigarettes. He talked about how the Latin Americans really knew how to fuck. He was much more sophisticated than I was, than any of us. He was a little jaundiced because of it. He was surrounded by a great deal of boyish enthusiasm and sincerity, and it disgusted him. I was very gratified, I remember, that Hermann liked, or tolerated, me at all. Even though I thought he was a bit of a... well.

Beat.

We were in science class. We were cutting up beetles and looking at the insides of them, and Hermann said something like "That's what your father did to the Jews." It was a sort of... joke. I was surprised, I didn't get the joke. I asked him about it. Here's what Hermann said to me.

Transition. It's 1963. RUDI and HERMANN are in science class at the German-language school in Asunción, Paraguay.

HERMANN   It's an analogy.

Beat.

An analogy, a parallel? I'm not saying it's an accurate analogy, but it's close enough that I thought you might react, for instance, with emotion—

9

RUDI   What are you talking about?

HERMANN   Your father. My father commanded in Poland, it's
            not as though he was some sort of war hero either, all
            right.

RUDI   What are you talking about.

HERMANN   Your father. Am I going too fast for you?

RUDI   What about my father?

HERMANN   It's as though he took a shit in the middle of the floor,
            and there's a dinner party going on, so we're all trying
            to pretend he didn't take a shit there, or at least, that it
            was all right to take a shit there. Again, not a fantastic
            analogy but just to be crude about it.

RUDI   I don't know what you're talking about.

HERMANN   Your father. During the war. Don't you... know about
            the war?

RUDI   Know what?

                 Beat.

HERMANN   Forget it, I don't know why I'm— Just, here, fill in the
            chart, I'll get rid of the tray—

RUDI   Hermann!

HERMANN   Or, fine, I'll fill in the chart, but we both know you're
            better at it.

RUDI   My father served in the army, during the war.

HERMANN   Yes. That's—yes. That's what he told you?

RUDI   Yes that's what he told me!

           Beat.

           What!? Hermann, what? What are you talking about?
           You're talking about my father. You're saying my
           father...? What are you saying?

           Beat.

           Tell me what you're saying.

           RUDI gets hold of him.

           Tell me what you're saying!

HERMANN   Your father was an SS doctor!

           RUDI lets him go.

           Did you know that? You didn't know that?

RUDI   He—no! He was a troop physician, in Russia, then he
           was promoted to captain, went back east, served as an
           officer...?

HERMANN   Yes...

RUDI   What?!

HERMANN   No, he—yes he went back east, he was... transferred to
           the... camps.

RUDI   The camps.

HERMANN   The camps, yes, the trains, on the ramp, selections? To the left, to the right? You know what Auschwitz is, don't you?

A reaction that indicates RUDI sort of knows, but isn't sure.

The camp? With the Jews? Doctors, experimenting— it's why you're so good at science, you got his...

Beat.

He probably also served at some of the work camps. You don't get sent to Auschwitz right away. There were doctors who killed themselves there, SS doctors; you had to have the right temperament for it so they were careful who they sent—

RUDI   He wasn't in the SS. *(off HERMANN's look)* He wasn't in the SS! His jacket, his military jacket is Wehrmacht—

HERMANN   He probably exchanged his SS uniform for an army jacket when the Allies were close to Berlin. "The Russians are coming! The Russians are coming!" "Here, lend me your jacket."

RUDI   No. No, it's his jacket, it fits him, it's his—

HERMANN   Then he kept an old jacket.

Beat.

I don't know, from watching... you, I get the sense you're not... stupid—don't you wonder why you're in Paraguay?

RUDI   We lost the war!

HERMANN   If—listen—if everyone who lost the war *left* Germany, there wouldn't be anyone *in* Germany, would there?

RUDI   This is stupid, there's no way my father…! Are you saying he—in the camps he—but if he was a doctor—I don't understand.

>   *Beat.*

There's no way my father…!

HERMANN   Then forget it.

>   *Transition. HERMANN is gone.*

RUDI   This was a big turning point in my relationship with my father. (*RUDI laughs.*) There are, I suppose, other things one can find out about one's father. That he fucks the maid, for instance. Hermann's father fucked the maid, or, rather, maids. My father didn't. My father never did anything unseemly in his life.

>   *Beat.*

Except, of course, he conducted a series of experiments on Jewish prisoners at Auschwitz between the summer of 1942 and the autumn of 1944.

>   *Beat.*

Injected them with typhus. For instance.

>   *Beat.*

There were no typhus cases on the hospital block, he wanted to study typhus, he injected four Dutch Jews with typhus.

Beat.

He operated on a series of women. With minimal anaesthetic and no surgical training, he removed their... ovaries— This is all familiar enough to you, though, isn't it?

Beat.

Then, my father took a series of detailed notes on his experiments, which he hoped would advance our understanding of human pathology, and would contribute to the growing pool of scientific knowledge, which has, to a great degree, become synonymous with "progress."

Beat.

Which, I have to say, is a lot worse than fucking the maid. It is so much worse than fucking the maid that it has... revolutionized our notion of evil.

Beat.

That's my father.

Beat.

You see. You see now why I smoke, I think I'm entitled.

Beat.

So, Paraguay, and I'm seventeen, and I'm at school. I'm impatient, pacing, it's after science class, I smoked a cigarette, and I stood on the front steps and waited for Hermann, who I was planning to—what's a euphemism for "kill"? "Resettle." (*RUDI laughs.*) No, I wanted to talk to

Hermann about what he'd said in science class, and so I stood on the front steps and waited for him, and waited, and when he didn't come out, I went to his house.

Transition. HERMANN *and* RUDI *are in* HERMANN's *bedroom.* RUDI *slammed the door as he entered and now they are standing still, looking at one another.*

HERMANN   Would you like something to drink? Or do you... just want to hit me?

Beat.

I don't mind being hit, but it's a little agonizing waiting like this.

Beat.

I'm going to get you a book to look at, all right? It's on my shelf. I'm going to go to my shelf, and get you a book. I had it shipped here, from Germany, it's in German, or you can just... look at the pictures.

Beat.

Can I get you the book?

RUDI   Just...!

HERMANN stays where he is and waits. Beat.

HERMANN   I suppose my father let you in, he's not very... welcoming, so I'm sorry if he... Anyway, welcome, you're... here, it's nice to have you... here, even though it's... under these—

RUDI   (*low*) He worked in...

Beat.

HERMANN   He... worked in...?

RUDI   Before he bought the pharmaceutical company, he worked in... it was the hospital, in Sajonia. He has medical journals, of his, in his study, that I... I looked at, but, the journals, they weren't from the hospital, they were...

HERMANN   From...? Of...?

RUDI nods.

Oh. *(off RUDI's look)* All right. Jesus. Cheer up. Have a cigarette, or would you like a drink? I have a bottle of whisky.

RUDI   You have photographs?

HERMANN goes and gets the book from where he's hidden it.

HERMANN   Here.

RUDI   What is it?

HERMANN   *Letters to a Young Poet.* I'm joking. It's a book about the final solution. It's called *The Final Solution.* Of the Jews? There's a photograph in here somewhere, if I can find it...

HERMANN flips through the book. He shows photographs to RUDI.

This is the ramp.

Beat.

The hospital block.

Beat.

(off RUDI's *look)* Corpses.

Beat.

Here's the photograph I wanted to... This is from 1943. That's the camp commandant, at Auschwitz, Rudolf Franz Hoess, and the chief doctor, Edward Wirths, and beside him on the left, that's your... father.

RUDI grabs the book.

Take the book.

Beat.

I'm sorry. I shouldn't have... told you like that, in class— I wanted to... make you—I think you're... very... not like the other—I don't know. I don't know. I'm sorry.

Beat.

Just, try to calm down before you see him, for fuck's sake.

Transition. HERMANN *is gone.*

RUDI   I went home. My father was on the front lawn, kneeling down, looking at the grass. It was dying a little around the edges, and he was telling one of the servants to water it again. He asked me how my school day was. I asked him how he liked it at Auschwitz.

Beat.

I remember the sound of blood in my ears, and my father calling to me as I walked into the house.

Beat.

He came after me.

Beat.

I stood there in the front hallway and asked my father questions about the war. They were the first real questions I'd ever asked about it.

Beat.

I told him I wanted to know about the mistakes he made at the camps.

Beat.

He didn't answer. He just... stood there and looked at me, with his... pink eyelids, and his well-manicured nails, and the slight stoop in his shoulders.

Beat.

I called him a murderer.

Beat.

He told me not to raise my voice.

Beat.

We had a... physical fight. I hit him a couple of times. I blacked his eye and I split his lip. He was mostly just trying to defend himself, he didn't hit me back, he just... turned towards the wall, and... let me hit him.

Beat.

My mother was screaming in the background the whole time.

Beat.

Afterwards, she kept saying, "What happened, what happened?" My father said, "It's over, it's fine, it's over."

Beat.

He... needed an X-ray, he was breathing badly, he thought I might have fractured one of his ribs, so I... drove him to the hospital. I remember the hospital, dirty little hallways and no doctors, my mother and father sitting there, on the metal chairs, her arms around him, his nose all crusted with blood.

Beat.

He looked very... beaten. (*RUDI laughs.*) He was already fifty-one years old, then.

Beat.

Later, I took the car and I went back to Hermann's house. The lights were all out. I—I put my fist through his bedroom window. I meant to knock on it, to get Hermann's attention, but I, well—

Transition. RUDI and HERMANN are standing outside of HERMANN's house. RUDI holds his hand as though he has cut it.

HERMANN   You just *broke* my window.

      Beat.

You're not going to hit me, are you? Because if you are, I want to take my glasses off.

      Beat.

Are you going to hit me?

      Beat.

You've cut your hand. You should get someone to look at your hand.

      Beat.

What happened? You hit him? You punched him?

      Beat.

You hit him.

      Beat.

Is he all right?

      Beat.

Where is he? Is he in hospital?

      Beat.

Is he all right?

Beat.

Don't... cry.

Beat.

Don't cry, it's all right.

> *HERMANN puts a hand on RUDI's shoulder. RUDI shrugs him off, then turns and hugs him with a sort of violence. RUDI cries in HERMANN's arms. Transition. HERMANN is gone.*

RUDI   I was upset. He *is* my...

Beat.

And, as a child, his child...

Beat.

There are some, of course, some childhood—he read Goethe to me, and well, *Mein Kampf*. I'm joking, he didn't read me *Mein Kampf*. He sent me to the German-language school, in Asunción, and we learned quotes from *Mein Kampf*, but my father, he read me children's books, *The Little Prince*, *Max and Moritz*...

Beat.

You don't want to hear this, do you? That he was a good father?

Beat.

(trying to remember what he was saying) I... found out about my father, in Paraguay, at seventeen, and then... what happened? Things fell apart for a period. They, yes, fell apart. But here's what really fucked me up.

Beat.

Life continued. My father wore his black suits to work, fucked my mother once a week, and at night he ate a good dinner. Then he fell asleep in his study with the radio on and the newspaper over his head. The servants watered the lawn twice a week instead of only once. The grass looked very green, and my father stood outside and admired it.

Beat.

Aside from the injuries, the split lip and the bruises to his eye, life just... continued. I didn't hit him again. The servants wiped the blood off the wallpaper in the front hallway.

Beat.

I asked him questions about it, after that. We ate dinner together every night at seven o'clock, so that was when I would argue with him about it. I would say things to him like, "How could you...?" I don't know, I was reading about the concentration camps in the books Hermann lent me, and I would say to him: "How could you"—one thing or another. "How could you do the selections?" That's the sort of thing I— "How could you select people?"

Beat.

He said, "All the doctors had ramp duty, all of us. No one liked it, but if we hadn't done it, it would have been chaos on the ramp, much worse."

Beat.

When I pushed him to say how he could select people for the gas chambers, he said, "You don't understand, we selected for the camp. If we hadn't selected people, they would have all gone on the transports, all of them. We selected based on the camp's labour requirements, that was it."

Beat.

I asked him: "Why would you go to the camp?"

Beat.

He said, "I was transferred there. After I was wounded in Russia, I was accepted into the Waffen-SS, and they transferred me."

Beat.

I asked him: "Then why did you stay there?"

Beat.

He said, "I wanted to leave, when I went there, and saw it. I was shocked and I wanted to leave. But my colleagues told me not to be stupid, I would become accustomed to it. And it would have been very bad for me to leave, for my career. For the superior who recommended me, it would have been very unpleasant. And for your mother, in Berlin, I had her there, I had a wife.

Beat.

Once, he said, "I took an oath to Hitler."

Beat.

When I asked him about the… experiments, he said something like, "You have to understand, it was nothing, there, to conduct those experiments, not even worth talking about. They were all going to go on a transport at some point, so it was nothing. And you can't imagine the… opportunity. Under any other circumstances it would not have been possible to use human subjects like that. I was able to do medical work, gain surgical experience, you should understand this, you're a scientist. If I learned about typhus then we could control it in the camps and on the Eastern Front, I could contribute to German medical literature, to the war, that way."

Beat.

Then he would go on and on about how I didn't understand, I didn't realize, those were different times.

Beat.

I would end up yelling, "How could you stay there, how could you stay there," and he would clutch his cutlery, and slump over his plate, and my mother would say, "Don't yell at him, look at him, you're upsetting him."

Beat.

One time, my mother pulled me out into the hallway during dinner and said, "Your father was wounded at the front, he was shot there, in Russia. I didn't want him to be sent back, I knew he would be killed if he was sent back, and I would be a widow, with nothing. I begged him to stay at the camp, because it was so much safer there."

Beat.

I think she felt that explained it.

Beat.

The point is, it went on and on like that, the fights over dinner, us going through the same set of questions over and over again, until finally, I just stopped arguing with him. I stopped arguing with him, and... life continued.

Beat.

I don't know. I don't know what I should have done. Turned him in?

RUDI regards the audience.

Yes? Turned him in?

Beat.

I do know that that was when I—those quiet dinners when I wasn't questioning him anymore, and the cutlery would clink, and the servants would come in and out, that's when I started to feel... guilty, because I...

Beat.

I was sitting across from my father over dinner and watching him talk and swallow food and laugh, and I was starting to... recognize him. I hadn't recognized him since I found out. He could have been anyone, sitting there across from me, but then I started to go back, to see him as... my... so I wanted to—I couldn't live that way, so I needed to...

RUDI regards the audience.

You'll like this part.

Beat.

Hermann, my friend Hermann, became a means of—a means of—well. The rumours were—we'd all heard them, but I was close with him, so I knew.

Beat.

Hermann became a means of...

Beat.

You have to remember. I was searching for a way of distancing myself from my father.

Beat.

It was Hitler's birthday. My father—all the old Nazis—celebrated Hitler's birthday at the beer hall every year. It was the only times my father let himself get drunk, Christmas and Hitler's birthday. While he was out celebrating, Hermann came to my house and I... took him into my father's study.

Transition. RUDI and HERMANN are in RUDI's father's study. HERMANN pours drinks for them.

HERMANN	"I want my youth to be strong and beautiful." Who said that?
RUDI	J.F. Kennedy?
HERMANN	No, stupid, *Hitler*. It's Hitler's birthday, why would I quote Kennedy?

Beat.

My father calls me down to his study every year on Hitler's birthday, and shakes my hand. Me, and then the servants. He talks to me just like I'm a servant, these days.

RUDI	No he doesn't.
HERMANN	He does, there's a girl here, the cook's daughter, she works somewhere up in Mexico, some family up there, she comes down to visit her mother. She's here now, she makes me things in the kitchen, bitter drinks that taste sort of like fruit and, well, shit, and these dry biscuits that I politely choke down. She comes and finds me, and gives these things to me and then runs away and hides. I couldn't work it out. Then I heard how my father talks to her. It's exactly how he talks to me. Like I'm a stranger he's obligated to look after. I think the girl must feel sorry for me.
RUDI	We all feel sorry for you, Hermann.

Beat.

HERMANN	He didn't call me down this year. I went by his study, after school, and the door was closed. I wonder if there's anything specific, or if I'm just *generally* disappointing him—pass me that.

RUDI passes HERMANN the cigarette. HERMANN takes a drag.

I'd like to go up there, to Mexico. I wonder what it's like up there. I'd like to go and walk around in the desert up there.

RUDI   Visit the girl?

Beat.

HERMANN   There's a picture of Hitler on your father's desk.

RUDI   Yes.

HERMANN   In a gold frame, that's nice. That's really nice, a picture of you and a picture of Hitler.

RUDI   It was a gift.

HERMANN   From whom?

RUDI   Hitler.

Beat.

HERMANN   What would you have done? Do you ever think about that?

RUDI   About what?

HERMANN   You know, the party tells you how bright your future is, and if you'll only go and work in a "special camp" for "prisoners" they'll promote you to Hauptman. I don't know what I'd do.

Beat.

	I would go.
RUDI	You wouldn't go.
HERMANN	I would.
RUDI	No, you wouldn't.
HERMANN	Why not?
RUDI	Your asthma? Your glasses? You cry when you get dirty.
HERMANN	Fuck you—you would go. You would have been *Sieg Heiling* along with the rest of them. Waffen-SS, Luftwaffe—
RUDI	Yeah.
HERMANN	Gestapo.
RUDI	Yeah, that's right, Gestapo.
HERMANN	You would have. You know you would. You're German, up and down.
RUDI	And you're Latin American?
HERMANN	I have a Latin American spirit.
RUDI	Because you can't play sports?
HERMANN	*(sarcastic)* Yes, exactly, because I can't play sports, that's why they've given me a passport.
	Beat.

Let's go, let's go out. Let's go drive around, I hate it here, in his study, what does he do in here?

RUDI   There's liquor here.

HERMANN   There's liquor out there.

RUDI   Where?

HERMANN   I don't know.

            Beat.

RUDI   To... one of the clubs. To one of the clubs you go to, is that where you want to go?

            Beat.

            Will you... take me to one of the clubs?

HERMANN   Why?

RUDI   Let's—show me... I know you... show me what you do?

            RUDI hits on HERMANN.

HERMANN   Don't—

RUDI   Show me.

HERMANN   You're drunk.

RUDI   I'm not—I'm yes—I'm drunk.

            RUDI hits on HERMANN again.

            Just let me.

HERMANN pushes RUDI away.

HERMANN   You don't—you're—this is stupid. You're drunk!

RUDI   I'm not drunk! I'm too nervous to be drunk. Let me.
You want to, I know you… I know you… like me.

>   *RUDI kisses HERMANN. They kiss more intensely. HERMANN undoes*
>   *RUDI's belt. He goes down on him. RUDI throws his head back.*
>   *RUDI turns and regards the audience.*

Well?

>   *Transition. HERMANN is gone.*

It's a nice image, isn't it? The two sons of prominent
Nazis sucking each other off in Paraguay somewhere?

>   *Beat.*

When my father found us he was… upset. (*RUDI laughs.*)
I heard the door to the study open, I looked up,
and there he was, in his black suit, standing in the
doorway.

>   *Beat.*

I… kept on… with Hermann, I didn't stop. It's a
bizarre thing, because your immediate reaction to a
parent seeing you have sex is to stop, and I had to fight
that for a moment, but then I was able to continue.

>   *Beat.*

He just stood there in the doorway, and watched.

>   *Beat.*

He closed the door on his way out.

Beat.

And then, of course, things fell apart. They fell apart, and not just for me, but for my father as well.

Beat.

He wouldn't look at me, he wouldn't speak to me, he wouldn't say my name. He passed me in the hallways with his eyes down. My mother locked herself in her room and cried. The sound filled the house. I would go out and come home to it. It went on and on like that, for weeks, their shame and my... well. Although, I wasn't as enthusiastic about it, after that.

Transition. RUDI and HERMANN are in RUDI's bedroom. HERMANN kisses RUDI. RUDI is not responding.

HERMANN What.

Beat.

What.

RUDI Just... I don't know.

RUDI breaks away. He lights a cigarette.

HERMANN What.

Beat.

Use language. That's what it's for.

Beat.

It's hot out there, hot and dry, but I suppose you wouldn't know because you haven't left the house.

Beat.

(*frustrated*) Something about your father.

RUDI   It's just, when I think about what he's been through, Berlin, and the Allies closing in, losing the war, Nuremburg, all his friends executed or handed over to the Russians to be killed or tortured, or, what do the Russians do?

HERMANN   Kill, torture.

RUDI   Then Paraguay, running a pharmaceutical company in some spic colonial outpost, that was fine. The Führer was still the Führer and *Deutschland über alles*.

HERMANN   (*referring to the cigarette*) Pass me that.

RUDI   And now he's...! He's eating dinner, when he eats it, with the servants in the kitchen. With the servants. And he hasn't stopped working for weeks. Works late, he's probably raking in the profits, the grosses are up because of me. His employees must wonder what the fuck is going on, this fit of enthusiasm for work suddenly—

HERMANN   Yes, well it's working, isn't it?

RUDI   What is?

HERMANN   Your experiment.

Beat.

Look, forget it. Where is he now?

RUDI   Downstairs.

HERMANN   Then he'll be sure to hear.

> *HERMANN kisses him. RUDI hardly responds, holds his cigarette.*
> *HERMANN stops, leans back, looks at him. Beat.*

RUDI   I told him I want to leave.

HERMANN   Leave.

RUDI   Leave, yes. Get out of the house, out of the country, if
            possible.

HERMANN   Out of the... country?

RUDI   I told him I would go to Germany.

HERMANN   Germany. Why?

RUDI   Why not?

HERMANN   Good, well, that's nice, you'll be able to keep up your
            German, and perhaps visit relatives? Go see where
            your father grew up, worked, met your mother. Wasn't
            that at Wannsee?

RUDI   I'm not *going* to Germany. I'm *leaving* Paraguay.

> *Beat.*

            ODESSA will fund it if I go to Germany. I don't want
            him to pay for it, and I don't want to stay here, so,
            Germany.

> *Beat.*

HERMANN   You're going to... leave? You're going to leave me...
          here?

RUDI   *(not sad to leave him)* I'll be sad to leave you, but, on the
          whole, Paraguay's a shithole, really.

          Beat.

          I went by his study, an hour ago, told him, "I want to
          leave." He was working on his—I don't know—accounts,
          anyway, he kept working, told me he would "make the
          arrangements"—

HERMANN   Well, what did you think would happen? You thought
          he would... what? Shake your hand?

RUDI   No, I—

HERMANN   Give you a fucking medal? *(off RUDI's look)* Well?

          Beat.

RUDI   Anyway, I'm leaving—

HERMANN   Leave, then! Go to Germany, New York, Jerusalem!
          Your father's a war criminal. It's going to be like this
          your whole life. You're going to spend half your time
          wanting him to die in a car crash so you can piss on his
          grave, and the other half scared he'll get extradited.
          Look at you. You've done this to piss him off, or, I
          don't know, shame him, and now—

RUDI   *(under HERMANN's line)* —no, it was to—

HERMANN   —that you've done it... yes it was.

RUDI   No, I didn't, it was to—

35

HERMANN   Yes, it was, in his study, on the fucking floor—

RUDI   No, I—no, I... meant to, yes, to—

HERMANN   What?

RUDI   To...

> *Beat.*

> (*sarcastic*) Yes, I—yes, this is what I thought would happen, I thought he would be like this, I thought he would—

HERMANN   But now "it's happened," you're all—

RUDI   No, I'm—I'm just—I don't know.

> *Beat.*

> I don't know!

> *Beat.*

HERMANN   (*more gently*) He's your father, you have to... You want him to be... proud of you, it's not... it doesn't make you guilty, or, like him, you're nothing like him—

> *HERMANN touches RUDI. RUDI shrugs him off violently.*

> Well, you're a little like him.

RUDI   You're nothing like your father; I can't say that, I'm not a fucking...

> *Beat.*

> I'm not a...

Beat. HERMANN walks to the door. RUDI runs and blocks his way, gets hold of his arms.

But my father thinks I am, so that's something, isn't it, Hermann? Hunh? That's something, isn't it? My father thinks I'm like you, so that's something?

Beat.

Lucky you. You'll never be like your father.

HERMANN gets RUDI off of him, and exits. HERMANN slams the door on his way out. Transition. RUDI regards the audience.

I was a little... confused, back then. Poor Hermann. But, he would easily find another...

Beat.

I left. I was seventeen, eighteen, by then, and I went to West Berlin, to Europe. I had a German passport and I went. ODESSA funded me to go to Germany. I—yes—accepted money from a Nazi organization, but I thought better I have it than whoever else they're...!

Beat.

I took very little with me when I left, very few... keepsakes.

Beat.

I went by the name on my German passport, after that, which perhaps you'll remember was "Otto Henrick." Not that my father's name is particularly remarkable, it's not a household name like Eichmann, or Mengele. Hitler. I just didn't want to use it.

Beat.

After that, a period of almost happiness. A period of...

Beat.

When I arrived in West Berlin, I rented rooms in the American sector, enrolled at Berlin's Free University, threw myself into my studies.

Beat.

Well, no, there was a brief period of— I was in occupied Germany, I saw all the bombed-out buildings, the Soviet soldiers my mother was terrified of when I was growing up, the Berlin Wall, the Reichstag. I walked around this... city that was so... familiar.

Beat.

But after that I threw myself into my studies. I took sciences, chemistry, and biology, played to my strengths. I tried to behave like any ordinary student, to live for the future. And West Berlin, Germany, was so disordered, so broken then—the Americans, the Soviets—that I could go unnoticed. I was just another anonymous post-war German. I didn't like to talk about the war, but then, who did?

Beat.

I got into the habit of referring to my parents in the past tense. At some point, someone asked me how it had happened. I said "car accident," and after that I just... kept saying it.

Beat.

I had a set of friends I spoke to about surface things. No politics, no history. I didn't join any of the student groups. I dated a series of nondescript blonds. I favoured classes taught by young professors, who qualified after the war. I was a good student, I worked hard, threw myself into it. When I wasn't studying, I was drinking. It was like three years of white noise. In my final year, I scored the highest in my class.

Beat.

My professors recommended medicine. (*RUDI laughs.*) Kept saying it, "Take medicine, you're right for it, the right temperament."

Beat.

"Congratulations on those scores, you're not going to go into business, I hope, not with those scores."

Beat.

"I'll write your reference letter for you, I know the head of the medical department, I'm sure they'll accept you."

Beat.

"My brother's a doctor, why don't you take a beer with him on the weekend, he'll tell you what the career is like…"

RUDI regards the audience.

What do you suppose I did?

Beat.

I applied for medical school. I was accepted into the university's Faculty of Medicine, and in the fall, I began attending classes.

Beat.

I was... a very good medical student. It quickly became apparent that I had a natural aptitude for it. I was often singled out by my professors. I was envied by the other students. Admired.

Beat.

Yes, that's right. I was very good at it. Good at labs. Good at exams. Also, I found I was never the one vomiting into the water fountain outside the auditorium.

Beat.

In my white coat.

Beat.

My father wore a white coat, over his SS uniform, in the camps.

Beat.

In my second term, I assisted in the dissection of a corpse. Four of us, three German physicians, and me, standing around the corpse of... this man, and I helped... dissect him, and I thought, I can't—this is what my father—I can't...

Beat.

The trains, over and over again I saw... myself on the ramp.

Beat.

I dropped out of medical school.

Beat.

I dropped out, and I didn't—I just—there was a long period of nothing, of... subsistence.

RUDI lights a cigarette.

I smoked a lot of cigarettes. (*RUDI laughs.*) There were cigarette burns in my rooms. I would find I... didn't want to move; I would be lying on the floor and I didn't want to move, so I would put my cigarette out where I was. I lost my deposit on those rooms because of that, because of all the cigarette burns in the carpet.

Beat.

I cashed my ODESSA cheque once a month.

Beat.

I walked around the city.

Beat.

I wondered if my whole life was going to be like this, a sort of doomed flight.

Beat.

And that's when I met her, Sarah Kleinman. I met her in the German Federal Archive. I had taken to going into libraries, archives, and circling my father's name in war documents, survivors' testimonies, the Nuremberg Trial transcripts. I was looking through deportation and transport records, and she—well—introduced herself.

Transition. RUDI and SARAH are in the German Federal Archive in West Berlin. RUDI is kneeling in the middle of a pile of papers.

SARAH   You're smoking in the archive.

          Beat.

RUDI   I'm sorry?

SARAH   You're smoking in the archive.

          Beat.

RUDI   I'll... put it out.

SARAH   No, no, I'm not an archivist.

RUDI   What are you then?

SARAH   I'm researching here, as well, in the archive, and I see you sitting here, on the floor, with those documents. You smoke about an inch away from them and ash onto the floor. Are they of interest?

RUDI   What?

SARAH   Those documents.

RUDI   Yes.

Beat.

SARAH   You seem to be spending a lot of time, on the floor, with those documents, and I wondered if... you've found what you're looking for?

Beat.

RUDI   I'm sorry?

SARAH   Are you looking for...?

Beat.

Last week there was a man from Norway. He sat there, just like you, in the aisle, until he found the record of it, of the transport.

Beat.

RUDI   Of the... I'm sorry, you're researching here, as well?

SARAH   I'm—yes—I'm looking through housing records. I had family in Berlin, so they must have had... housing. But, I came here first, to this section, I found my... mother here, found the record of a transport on the date when I know she went east.

RUDI   East.

SARAH   Yes.

RUDI   To the camps?

SARAH   Yes?

RUDI   You...? You're...? Are you...? Are you...? I'm sorry,
            are you... a...? You're saying you had family who were
            deported to...?

SARAH   You... didn't have family... who were—?

RUDI   No. No, my family... no.

SARAH   You're... German?

RUDI   Yes.

            Beat.

            I'm... sorry, there aren't many of you who stayed,
            who—after the war—

SARAH   No, we didn't feel... all that welcome.

RUDI   Yes. No.

SARAH   And we didn't stay. We moved to the States. (*off RUDI's
            look*) The United States of America—

RUDI   I—yes, but when?

SARAH   In 1945, when the Allies liberated the camps. She met
            my father. He was with the 14th Armoured. He found
            her at one of the displaced persons camps, and they
            fell in love. It's an unlikely backdrop for love, post-
            war Germany, but they did somehow manage to fall in
            love, and they were married and my mother emigrated
            to the States.

RUDI   Is your father also... a—

SARAH   Yes?

RUDI   Your mother... survived the camps?

            SARAH nods.

            Which one?

SARAH   Auschwitz.

            Beat.

            And your parents? During the war?

RUDI   They were—my father was—he was, yes—a National
            Socialist. He was—*I'm* not. I'm studying Jews—Jewish—
            so, I'm researching here—

SARAH   He served in the war?

RUDI   He was a medic, a troop physician, yes. With the—he
            was in Russia, mostly, Eastern Front. And then, after
            the war, he worked in pharmaceuticals, until he...
            There was an accident. On the Autobahn.

SARAH   (*polite, but not sorry*) I'm sorry.

            Beat.

            And you're researching...?

RUDI   I'm researching, yes, he's... My father died, so I can't
            ask him if he was involved in the... resettlements, the
            deportations, in the... east.

SARAH   You think he might have been?

            Beat.

RUDI   Yes.

            Beat.

SARAH   My mother also... died, before I could ask her
            about... herself, her family, so I wanted to come
            here, see where she lived, see Germany. *(indicating*
            RUDI) Germans.

RUDI   I'm...! I'm very pleased to...! I'm pleased that you
            are—feel you want to—welcome!

SARAH   Thank you.

            Beat.

RUDI   Otto Henrick.

SARAH   Sarah Kleinman.

            They shake hands awkwardly because RUDI doesn't know what to
            do with his cigarette. Transition. SARAH is gone. RUDI regards the
            audience.

RUDI   Sarah was... *Jewish,* so that was odd. That was very odd
            and also... exhilarating. She was the first Jew I'd met.
            I'd only ever seen photographs. And... anatomical
            sketches in my father's... medical...

            RUDI looks away.

            Sarah's mother, Inge Rosenthal, was deported to
            Auschwitz on September 3, 1943. My father was...
            there, at the camp, at that time. So, yes.

            Beat.

It wasn't exactly a premeditated... but, after that, I did—I know I did—I spent a lot of time helping Sarah to use the archives, and, well, following her around, so I suppose it's not so surprising that the desire to know her, to... apologize to her... on behalf of my...

Beat.

When I left Paraguay, I took one... keepsake... (*RUDI laughs.*) of my father's with me. I told Sarah I had it, at my apartment, and she... wanted to see it.

> *Transition. RUDI and SARAH are in RUDI's Berlin apartment. RUDI is holding out his father's military jacket for SARAH to look at.*

SARAH   It's in good condition.

RUDI   Is it?

SARAH   He kept it all wrapped up?

RUDI   Yes, in the closet.

SARAH   There must be a lot of these jackets in closets and basements, in Germany, Austria, Poland.

> *Beat. RUDI lights a cigarette.*

This insignia is Brandenburg Division.

RUDI   Yes.

SARAH   They were smokers. Like you. The Germans who surrendered to my father's regiment were Brandenburg. He told me they were always begging for smokes.

Beat.

He's well decorated, for a non-combatant. He was a physician?

RUDI   Yes.

SARAH   This is the Iron Cross, Second Class. The Winter Campaign ribbon. A wound badge, he was wounded?

RUDI   Yes. In 1942, in the spring. A bullet wound, to the shoulder. Then he went back...

SARAH   East?

RUDI   Yes.

RUDI turns away, smokes.

SARAH   Do you have any photographs of him?

RUDI   No.

SARAH   No? None?

RUDI   We didn't... like each other very much, we didn't—I didn't keep many of his things. The jacket, yes, I kept the jacket, but—it's probably difficult for you to—if you don't have family who you dislike—

SARAH   *(shrugging)* I didn't like my mother all that much.

RUDI   No?

SARAH   No. Not much.

RUDI   Why?

SARAH   Why didn't you like your father?

RUDI   Well, because he's—because he was a... National
            Socialist—

SARAH   But as a child, would that...?

            Beat.

            Why did you keep this, then? Is it... a—? .

RUDI   No—

SARAH   —a sentimental—

RUDI   No, just a... no.

            Beat.

SARAH   Does it fit you?

RUDI   What, the jacket?

SARAH   Yes.

RUDI   When I was young, I tried it on. Now, I don't know.

            SARAH holds the jacket out to him. RUDI looks at SARAH, hesitates.

            (*referring to his cigarette*) Hold that.

            *SARAH takes his cigarette. She turns away while RUDI puts on the
            jacket. SARAH turns back around and looks at RUDI in the jacket.
            It fits him very well.*

            I don't think I can wear it out, though.

Beat. RUDI *takes the jacket off.*

SARAH Thank you for showing me the jacket.

RUDI Please.

  Beat.

  Would you like it?

SARAH Would I like to... have it?!

RUDI Yes.

SARAH I don't think I can take your father's jacket.

RUDI Why not? If you don't take it, a museum will have it. It seems right that you have it if you want it.

  Beat.

  Why don't I trade you for it?

SARAH Trade me for it?

RUDI Yes.

SARAH For what?

RUDI For—will you—I have tickets to the theatre? A play, I have two tickets to see a play. At the theatre.

SARAH You want to take me to the theatre in exchange for your father's Nazi jacket.

RUDI Yes. On Saturday. I wanted to... ask you to come—to... come with me.

SARAH   You're asking me on a date?

RUDI   Yes.

> *SARAH laughs. She stops, looks at RUDI.*

SARAH   What would your father say?

> *Beat.*

RUDI   What would yours?

> *Beat.*

You can just take the jacket.

SARAH   No, I—I'll come. It's a little perverse, but all right. I mean, the exchange is perverse, not the…

> *RUDI nods and laughs. So does SARAH.*

All right.

> *RUDI holds out the jacket. SARAH laughs. She takes the jacket.*

Thank you for the jacket.

> *SARAH exits. Transition.*

RUDI   All through that week, verses of Goethe's love poetry that I'd had to learn in school ran through my brain. That, the German romantic poetry, and some of Hitler's speeches, all joined together and sloshing around in my brain. I was also feeling guilt, in with the love poetry and Hitler's speeches, because—I suppose you've noticed—I was lying to Sarah about my father.

Beat.

I lied to her, when I met her at the archive, so that she would... let me talk to her, and also out of habit, I suppose. But it didn't seem right to lie to her anymore if she was going to let me take her on a date. On Saturday, we went to the theatre, and then I invited her back to my apartment, to tell her. I meant to tell her. But then, well—

> *Transition.* SARAH *and* RUDI *are in* RUDI*'s Berlin apartment. They kiss, and pull their clothes off. They are having sex on the floor, with their clothes on for the most part, as though sex overtook them before they undressed, and also it's perhaps the only kind of sex these two could have right now, less intimate, semi-clothed sex. They have sex for a beat.*

SARAH   Oh God.

RUDI   *(stopping and looking at* SARAH, *nervous)* Are you... all right?

SARAH   Yes?

> RUDI *closes his eyes tightly, and continues with determination. But now* SARAH *is thinking. She thinks, eyes open, for a moment.*

I feel... I feel—

RUDI   *(stopping, nervous)* What?!

SARAH   It's all right, isn't it?

RUDI   It's all right. It's, yes! It's—

SARAH   No. No, I mean—not the—but we're—it's—and somehow this feels all right.

RUDI   Yes!

SARAH   No, I mean—I'm being... No, I mean that we're—
              that it's you and I, and so few years later. Of course
              you're—I find you very—but because of the—I thought
              it would feel wrong. But it doesn't, it feels right.

                  Beat.

              As though it's this simple for us to talk and this act
              of... love is possible between us.

                  *Beat. SARAH remembers that RUDI is, at this moment, having sex
                  with her.*

              I'm sorry. You can keep going. Please. Keep going. It
              was nice. So was the play. I don't know why I'm talking
              so much.

RUDI   No, no, please, it's... I know what you're talking about.

SARAH   Do you?

RUDI   Yes. Of course. Just what you said.

SARAH   How does it feel to you?

RUDI   It feels, well, nice.

                  SARAH laughs. Transition. SARAH is gone.

              Yes, it felt nice, it felt very nice with Sarah, and here's
              why. I was in love with her. I was, fully, in love with
              her, even then, the first night in my apartment.

                  Beat.

You must see how appealing it...

> *Transition.* RUDI *and* SARAH *in* RUDI's *Berlin apartment. They drink glasses of whisky.* RUDI *has asked her to sing the* Sh'ma. *He's holding a prayer book.*

SARAH   *(singing)* Sh'ma Israel, Adonai Elochainu, Adonai Echad. Baruch shaim k'vod malchutainu le'olam va'ed. *(referring to the prayer book)* Where did you find this?

RUDI   Sing the—what was the first part that you sang?

SARAH   Where did you find this?

RUDI   At the flea market. I bought the book and a... prayer shawl, for two Deutschmarks, off this man, he told me he found them in his attic.

> *Beat.*

What was the first part of the prayer?

SARAH   *(speaking)* Sh'ma Israel, Adonai Elochainu—

RUDI   No. Sing it.

> *Beat.*

Sing it.

SARAH   *(singing quickly and unenthusiastically)* Sh'ma Israel, Adonai Elochainu, Adonai Echad. Read the Mourner's Kaddish. There's no mention of death in it, only God, it doesn't make any sense.

RUDI   Where is it?

SARAH	It's... here.

> *SARAH flips through the prayer book and shows him where it is.*
> *RUDI looks at it for a moment while SARAH pours herself more*
> *whisky.*

RUDI	Sing it.

SARAH	No.

RUDI	Sing it!

SARAH	I'm not singing it!

RUDI	Why not? Sing it, I want to hear it.

SARAH	You don't sing it. You say it. *Yit'gadal v'yit'kadash sh'mei raba. Amein.* Congregation answers, "Amein."

RUDI	*Amein.*

SARAH	*B'al'ma di v'ra khir'utei...* something, *mal'khutei b'chayeikhon uv'yomeikhon uv'chayei d'khol beit yis'ra'eil... ba'agala uviz'man kareev...*

> *SARAH kisses him.*

RUDI	No, you're stopping, why? Keep going. No!

SARAH	*(kissing RUDI)* I forget it.

RUDI	No... no! You don't! And, oh look, it's here, in the prayer book, all written out phonetically.

> *RUDI holds the prayer book out. SARAH looks at it. She starts to*
> *quickly recite the prayer, to pacify RUDI. At first SARAH recites it*

mechanically and impatiently, but as she recites it, it starts to have an affect on her.

SARAH   *Yit'gadal v'yit'kadash sh'mei raba. B'al'ma di v'ra khir'utei, v'yam'likh mal'khutei, b'chayeikhon uv'yomeikhon uv'chayei d'khol beit yis'ra'eil ba'agala uviz'man kariv v'im'ru: amein. Y'hei sh'mei raba m'varakh, l'alam ul'al'mei al'maya, yit'barakh v'yish'tabach v'yit'pa'ar v'yit'romam v'yit'nasei v'yit'hadar v'yit'aleh v'yit'halal sh'mei d'kud'sha, b'rikh hu. L'eila min kol bir'khata v'shirara toosh'b'chatah v'nechematah, da'ameeran b'al'mah, v'eemru: amein. Y'hei sh'lama raba min sh'maya v'chayim aleinu v'al kol yis'ra'eil v'im'ru: amein. Oseh shalom bim'romav hu ya'aseh shalom aleinu v'al kol Yis'ra'eil v'im'ru, amein.*

         SARAH is trying not to cry.

Amein.

         Transition. SARAH is gone.

RUDI   With Sarah, I felt that I—it was a religious—a superstitious feeling, I suppose, but I felt that there was a possibility for undoing some of what my father— not undoing, that's stupid, but that if my father stood on the ramp, then somehow with Sarah, loving Sarah, I was, yes, undoing his... I loved her and that was somehow... an act of... redemption or... I don't know, something was... closing, or...

         Beat.

With Sarah, I felt... less guilty. Like my father could be dead for all I...!

         Beat.

Later, we drove out to the camp together. We rented a car and crossed the checkpoint, in the American sector. The American soldiers joked with Sarah, wanted to know why she was wasting her time with a German. The Soviet soldiers weren't as good-humoured as the Americans, but we made it through all right, and then we drove through the GDR, the East Block, into Poland.

Transition. RUDI *and* SARAH *are in the parking lot at Auschwitz.* SARAH *is throwing up. She's crouched down and* RUDI *is hovering a foot or so away from her, holding her purse.*

Are you all right, Sarah, do want some water or... beer?

Beat.

(to check if she is all right) Sarah?

SARAH   I'm... yes, I'm just...!

Beat.

You just have to get on the highway. You just go east on the highway and... you're at Auschwitz. I don't know why I'm surprised, I looked at the map, but I am surprised, and now I'm throwing up.

Beat.

It's human, I suppose, the human element—

RUDI   Yes.

SARAH   No, not about throwing up, about vanity. I still feel it, even here. I'd still rather not throw up in front of you.

RUDI   I… like it.

SARAH   Yes, well, you say that, but you're never going to marry
            me now you've seen me throw up.

RUDI   Will you…

SARAH   What?

RUDI   Marry me?

SARAH   In the parking lot at Auschwitz.

RUDI   I mean, no, I mean, not here.

SARAH   Where?

RUDI   In a synagogue.

SARAH   No.

RUDI   Will you marry me?

SARAH   No.

RUDI   Why not?

SARAH   Because… you're a German.

RUDI   Is that why?

SARAH   Yes. Maybe, I don't know, could you find another time
            to ask me? I'm throwing up, at Auschwitz, and you're a
            fucking German, and also I think I'm pregnant.

RUDI   What?

SARAH	It's nothing, it's probably just because you drove so badly.
RUDI	Sarah!
SARAH	Come. Let's go back in there, and... finish the tour.

SARAH exits. Transition.

RUDI	We walked through the rest of the camp together. Well, not together, Sarah walked ten feet ahead of me for most of it. And, walking around, at the camp, I had a... vision... of my... family. Not my father, but of Sarah and I, and a child, and that seemed like... the most...

Beat.

My father would have a Jewish grandchild. (*RUDI laughs.*)

Beat.

Later, Sarah and I stood on the ramp together.

Transition. RUDI and SARAH are on the ramp at Auschwitz. A long beat of silence as they look out together at the train tracks. RUDI looks at SARAH, then SARAH looks at him. Transition.

The next day, we drove to Krakow and found a doctor who spoke some German. He tested Sarah's urine, and then we sat in the waiting room for three and half hours until he finally came back out and said, "Congratulations."

SARAH exits. Beat.

I spent most of the three-day drive back to West Germany trying to talk Sarah into marrying me. I wasn't particularly convincing. All I said was, "Please marry me," "Please marry me," over and over again.

Beat.

Back in West Berlin, in my apartment, we were still fighting about it, and the whole time we were fighting, there was a letter from Hermann lying on my desk. He'd found me somehow, through ODESSA, I suppose. I remember the letter because it was there, on my desk, while Sarah and I fought, and I kept thinking, "I should get rid of that," while Sarah told me again why she wouldn't marry me, why she didn't want the baby.

Transition. RUDI and SARAH are in RUDI's apartment in West Berlin.

SARAH   We can't just *have a baby*.

RUDI   Why not? That's how it happens. You just *have them*.

SARAH   We can't just *get married* and *have a baby*—

RUDI   Why not? We're already pretending to be married at hotels, it's the same, Sarah, only we're not pretending—

SARAH   I won't even fit into a wedding dress—

RUDI   —all you have to do is sign the papers—

SARAH   —I'll have to wear a big... curtain, or blanket or—

RUDI   You want a wedding dress?

SARAH   Yes!

RUDI   That's fine, I'll find you one.

SARAH   How?

RUDI   I'll go into the shops and tell them I knocked my
          girlfriend up and now I have to marry her, can they
          please *put her in a dress*?

                   Beat.

          If we get married in the next... few weeks, or months,
          then you'll be able to wear any wedding dress you like.

SARAH   Married... in a few weeks? I came here *for the summer*,
          I am *enrolled in courses*, in New York, in September, I
          am...! *(to herself)* Why did I come here? I didn't have to
          come here—

RUDI   *(under SARAH's line)* —Sarah—

SARAH   *(to herself)* —I could have stayed in New York.

RUDI   But you didn't, you came here, you wanted to come
          here, you met me—

SARAH   It's the stupidest possible reason to get married—

RUDI   I *want* the baby—

SARAH   No, not the baby, this!

RUDI   What?

SARAH   This!

RUDI   What?! I don't..?! What?

SARAH   This! This apartment. You have all this... Jewish...! That's not how to choose a wife—

RUDI   That's not why I love you—

SARAH   Yes it is—

RUDI   It's not...! It wasn't *any* Jewish girl, if all I wanted was a Jewish girl, then—

SARAH   How do you know?! You've never—

RUDI   Sarah—

SARAH   You haven't! You've never even met another...! Come to New York, then you could see if you love me, or if it's just—

RUDI   What about you? And your German...? You have a German collection, all those Nazi... that awful brooch, and those—

SARAH   That's my *point*, it's *both of us*, we're *both*...!

           Beat.

           It's not love, it's something else, curiosity, it's *like* love, but—

RUDI   Sarah! I love you, and that's not—you're a beautiful woman, by anyone's... It's not just—it's—(*sarcastic, off* SARAH'*s look*)—yes, yes, you're right, if you'd been some old—like that Austrian woman, at the archive, with lipstick all over her face, I would have loved you just because you were...! That's right.

           Beat.

SARAH   You like it that I'm Jewish—

RUDI   Yes, I do. *And* I love you.

        Beat.

SARAH   My father didn't want me to come here. He said, "Go
        to Paris, go to Jerusalem. Don't spend my money in
        Germany, why give it to the Germans?" And now, I'm
        supposed to call him and say…?

RUDI   That's the…? You don't want to call your father?

SARAH   No, that's not the only—

RUDI   I'll sit here with you, I'll dial—

        RUDI picks up the phone.

SARAH   I can't just… No! Don't!

RUDI   Once you do it—

SARAH   Just…! Don't!

        Beat. RUDI puts the phone down.

        My mother did this to him, she left him, and now I call
        and tell him… I'm…? Marrying a fucking German?

RUDI   Well, I wouldn't say it like that.

SARAH   How should I say it then?

        Beat.

RUDI   Your mother… left him?

SARAH   No, she...!

       Beat.

     (hard) She slit her wrists, in our bathtub, in our apartment in New York. So yes, she left.

       Beat.

     (hard) She was... depressed.

       Beat.

     (hard) He found her.

       Beat.

     There were flies in the cupboard, in our apartment. A fly infestation one winter, maggots in all the boxes of food, but she wouldn't throw any of it out. She made me eat a bowl of cereal from the cupboard that had maggots in it. And I'll be like that, as a mother—

RUDI   Sarah—

SARAH   — I'll be crazy, and God only knows what you'll be like, as a father. You'll—I don't know—deport it, because it's not blond, or because it's crippled, or you'll realize you hate it or—

RUDI   *(to stop her talking)* Sarah...!

SARAH   —we'll be terrible, awful—

RUDI   Sarah.

       RUDI holds her.

Sarah.

Beat.

In that shitty hotel, with the... wallpaper on the ceiling—I lay there and because of... this, I couldn't sleep, so I just sketched you, for hours. I traced your hands, I kept stopping—I thought the sound of the pencil was waking you up—

SARAH   *(low)* —we won't even be able to get married in *shul*, some civil servant will have to—

RUDI   You have very long fingers, very pale ones, with little nails on them, and the veins in your wrists are very blue.

Beat.

You love me.

Beat.

SARAH   Give me the phone.

> *RUDI goes and gets the phone. He hands it to SARAH, who dials.*
> *Transition.*

RUDI   Sarah's father... didn't like it. *(RUDI laughs.)* He didn't want us to come home, to New York , for the wedding; he didn't want to have anything to do with it. But, in the end, he travelled to West Berlin a week before the ceremony with two of Sarah's aunts.

Beat.

He spent most of his time, in West Berlin, in the hotel room, refusing to go out, refusing to speak to Sarah.

It was painful for her, to have them all ashamed of her like that, so she would come to my apartment during the days and leave them at the hotel by themselves.

Beat.

And of course I was still... struggling with... I didn't want to upset Sarah, so I still hadn't told her about my father. I'd had to lie a little more. Because of the wedding plans, I'd told Sarah that my ODESSA money was insurance from my parents' car accident, that I wasn't close with my family, I didn't keep in touch with any of them, they all lived in Strasbourg, that sort of thing.

Beat.

We'd arranged for a quick 7 a.m. civil ceremony, barely anyone attending. Sarah didn't like it. She wanted there to be someone there, on the groom's side.

Beat.

As it turns out...

Beat.

The ceremony was only two days away—Sarah's veil was pinned to the back of one of the armchairs in her hotel room to keep it from creasing—when Hermann arrived at my apartment.

> *Transition. HERMANN and SARAH are standing together in RUDI's Berlin apartment. HERMANN and SARAH are both smoking and drinking whisky. RUDI has just walked in. They all stare at each other for a moment.*

HERMANN   You've—you're—of course, you've broadened—you were young, and now you're…

RUDI   Hermann?

Beat.

You're—Hermann, you're here, you're… in Germany. You're—you've met Sarah? *(to SARAH)* Sarah, this is… Hermann. He's a childhood friend, an old…

RUDI looks at SARAH. He stops talking.

HERMANN   Sarah's been sitting here with me. She let me in, to your apartment, we've been drinking your whisky.

Beat.

I've been—yes—touring in Europe, aimlessly… touring, endless train stations, and cheap—so I thought I'd come to West Berlin. I hoped I might see you, it's been, what? Six, seven years since you… since we've seen each other.

SARAH exits, suddenly.

RUDI   *(calling as she leaves)* Sarah…!

The door slams in RUDI's face.

HERMANN   Yes, I thought that might happen. She was holding herself together quite well, for about a quarter of an hour, there, but when you came in…

Beat.

Poor thing.

Beat.

She seemed to think your father was dead, among other things. She didn't seem to know that you grew up in Paraguay. I slipped something about that, I said I was an old friend from Paraguay, and that seemed to confuse her, and then it got a little... awkward. I knew you'd changed your name, to Otto Henrick, isn't that right?

RUDI I—yes.

HERMANN But I didn't know you'd killed off your father.

Beat.

Your father is very well, in fact. He's still there, in the old neighbourhood. A few of them have switched countries, but not your father, he's still there. Mine isn't.

RUDI Where is he?

HERMANN Died in a car accident.

Beat.

Caught pneumonia, then broke his hip falling out of bed at the hospital, then went into a coma. He wanted to be buried here, in Germany. That's what was in his will, "Bury my remains in Berlin." I scattered his ashes in our swimming pool, before I left.

Beat.

Sarah. Not a lot of Sarahs in Berlin. Not a lot of... You've moved on from—to *Jews*, I take it. Well, your father would be...! But I suppose he doesn't know?

Beat.

She seemed very nice. I would say congratulations, but…

Beat.

If she forgives you, I'll rent a suit.

Beat.

I like it here, in Germany, I see why you stay. It seems right, to wait it out here, with all the other old… remnants of the war.

HERMANN puts his arms around RUDI and holds him.

Have you missed… Paraguay?

Beat.

No? Not happy to see me?

Beat.

Yes, that's… how *I* looked when *you* left.

Transition. HERMANN is gone.

RUDI   I went to Sarah's hotel. Sarah was there, in her room, by herself. She was… packing her suitcases.

RUDI turns as though he's about to enter the scene, then turns back, regards the audience.

I've… never told you my name, have I? I've never told you my… name. I don't like to… But, let me introduce myself.

Transition. RUDI and SARAH are in SARAH's hotel room.

SARAH   Rudolf Klausener.

        Beat.

        Your father's name is Rudolf Klausener, and that's your name.

RUDI   *(low)* Yes.

SARAH   Rudolf.

RUDI   *(nods)* Rudi.

        Beat.

SARAH   I'm leaving. I'm going back to New York. I'm going to leave with my father and go back to New York.

        Beat.

RUDI   *(low)* What about the baby—

SARAH   *(furious)* Oh, the baby! Oh no, the baby! Oh God, what about the baby!?

RUDI   Sarah, sit down.

        RUDI moves towards her. SARAH backs away.

        Is there something that I can do to... convince you to... sit down. Sarah, please, listen, I love you—

SARAH   Oh you love me, and the *baby*, and please sit down!

        Beat.

(*calmer*) He's... in Paraguay, somewhere, and you know where. You know where he is.

> *RUDI nods, or gestures to suggests he does.*

> *Beat.*

I'm leaving. I'm leaving with my father—

RUDI   Sarah—

SARAH   If I go back now, I can—I know a doctor in New York who can fix it for me, I'm not even ten weeks.

> *Beat.*

RUDI   That is—!

SARAH   (*calm*) What?

> *Beat.*

RUDI   Sarah, please—

SARAH   You didn't tell me, you... lied, you—

RUDI   No, I—

SARAH   You lied.

RUDI   No, I just didn't tell you. Because, Sarah, listen, when I was young, in Paraguay, Sarah, my father didn't tell me... about the camp, so when I met you, it was easy to just tell you what he'd told me.

SARAH   You're telling me lies your *father* told you.

Beat.

Why are you... *doing this*? Why are you...?

RUDI   I'm not! I'm not—it's not—!

SARAH   You told me he *was dead.*

RUDI   I have to say that because he's in Paraguay! He's a *war criminal*, hiding in Paraguay, I can't just...!

Beat.

SARAH   You love him.

Beat.

You do, you—

RUDI   No!

SARAH   You're—we talked about Eichmann together, the trial, we talked about—

RUDI   Sarah—

SARAH   And meanwhile—

RUDI   And—yes! And I'll—

SARAH   Meanwhile, he's *in Paraguay.*

RUDI   I'll call the...! What if I call the...? What if I turn him in, like Eichmann. What if I... turn him in?

Beat.

(*calmer*) What if I... turn him in?

Beat.

Then, would you—

SARAH   I don't know. I don't know anything. Why *would* I?

Beat.

RUDI   (*low*) Sarah.

SARAH   If you turn him in, then... when he is *standing trial*, when he is... in Jerusalem, standing trial.

Beat.

RUDI   (*low*) And the... the baby, will you...?

Beat.

Just wait, I'll—Sarah, I'll... please. I'll call you in New York, I'll tell you what... happens. Just wait, please— wait a week, don't...

Beat.

Sarah?

Beat.

Sarah?

Beat.

SARAH   I don't know what to... Rudi?

Transition. SARAH is gone.

RUDI   Well, you've just about understood, now, haven't you?

Beat.

I called the bureau, the Mossad, in Israel, I talked to a series of bureaucrats about extradition, told them what I knew, the house, the street, but it seems that extradition is a long process. (*RUDI laughs.*) I wouldn't be able to... go back to Sarah for... well, years, possibly. So I have to...

Beat.

He's a war criminal.

Beat.

And there isn't much to stop me from... other than my own... He is my... *father*, so I do have some... I am sorry to say, but I do... have some...

RUDI takes a handgun out of his suitcase.

They found it, at customs, the customs official with Band-Aids on his hands. I paid him off. That's Paraguay for you.

Beat.

Where's my mother, I wonder? Upstairs, or... out?

Beat.

So... now I just have to go in there and... do it.

RUDI tries to light a cigarette. He can't because his hands are shaking. He stops trying, throws the lighter and cigarette down.

These cigarettes aren't helping.

Beat.

There is no other solution to this... problem, other than to...

Beat.

This is the only solution, isn't it?

Beat.

And then I can go back to my... family.

Beat.

It's unpleasant, but...

Beat.

You think I should do it, don't you?

Beat.

You think I should do it?

Beat.

Yes?

Beat.

Yes.

RUDI *goes to the door. He looks back at us one more time. He opens the door. In the doorway he pauses. Then holds the gun up to his head.*

Blackout. End play.

ACKNOWLEDGEMENTS

My thanks are most of all due to Alisa Palmer. Her direction acted as dramaturgy and many of the play's scenes and moments were born in rehearsal. I am deeply indebted to my dramaturges Joanna Falck, Andy McKim, and Richard Rose, whose comments and insights shaped the script. Camellia Koo's beautiful design of *East of Berlin* influenced my writing decisions and should therefore be acknowledged here. I want to thank the actors who workshopped the first draft of the play: Matthew Edison, Brendan Gall, and Liisa Repo-Martell. I am very grateful to Paul Dunn, Diana Donnelly, and Brendan Gall, the three actors who premiered *East of Berlin*, for their immense contribution to the play's development. I also want to acknowledge Christian Barry and Noah Moscovitch for their informal dramaturgy. *East of Berlin* was developed through the Playwrights Unit at Tarragon Theatre.

I relied heavily on two books to create the psyches and circumstances of the characters in *East of Berlin*: *Born Guilty: Children of Nazi Families* by Peter Sichrovsky, and *Legacy of Silence: Encounters with Children of the Third Reich* by Dan Bar-On. Thank you also to the following works: Robert Jay Lifton's *The Nazi Doctors: Medical Killing and the Psychology of Killing*, Hannah Arendt's *Eichmann in Jerusalem: A Report on the Banality of Evil*, Primo Levi's *Survival in Auschwitz*, Elie Wiesel's *Night*, and Art Spiegelman's *Maus I* and *II*.

Hannah's past writing for the stage includes her short works *The Russian Play*, *Essay*, *USSR*, and *Mexico City*. Hannah's plays have been produced across the country, including at Alberta Theatre Projects, the Magnetic North Theatre Festival, Factory Theatre, and Tarragon Theatre, where she is currently playwright-in-residence. Hannah is a graduate of the National Theatre School of Canada's acting program and she attended the University of Toronto.